JOBS IN SPORT

PETER TURNER

WORKING IN AUSTRALIA

REDBACK publishing

First published 2023 by
Redback Publishing
Australia

www.redbackpublishing.com.au
orders@redbackpublishing.com.au

ISBN 978-1-761400-37-7 PBK

Author: Peter Turner
Editor: Caroline Thomas
Designer: Redback Publishing

Original illustrations © Redback Publishing 2024
Originated by Redback Publishing

A catalogue record for this book is available from the National Library of Australia

Acknowledgements
Abbreviations: l—left, r—right, b—bottom, t—top, c—centre, m—middle
We would like to thank the following for permission to reproduce photographs: (Images © shutterstock)

p24 Fotokostic / Shutterstock,
25br Steve Todd / Shutterstock,
27 WR studio / Shutterstock,
p27br Tomasz Koryl / Shutterstock,
p28 PQK / Shutterstock,

CONTENTS

WORKING IN SPORT

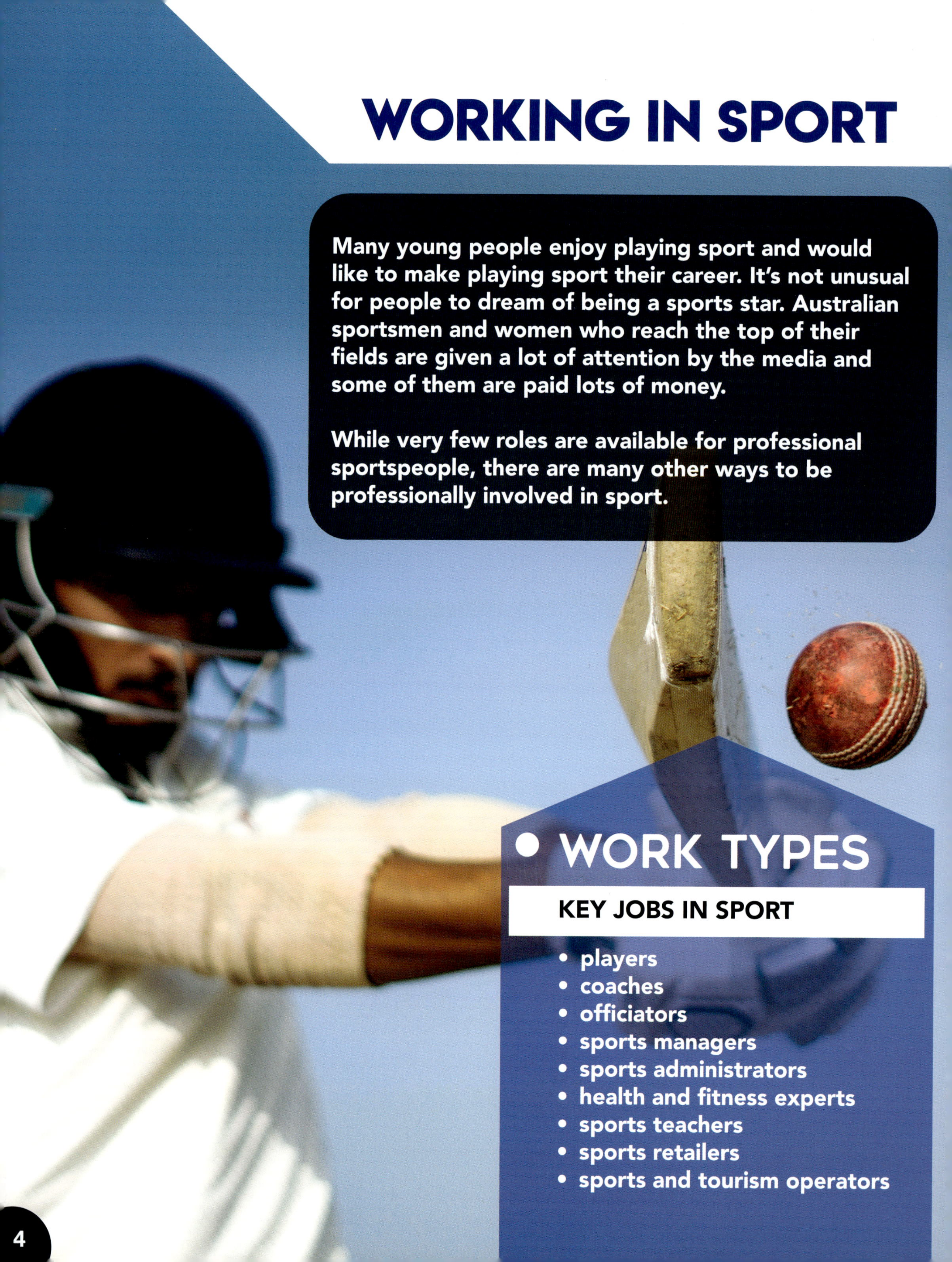

Many young people enjoy playing sport and would like to make playing sport their career. It's not unusual for people to dream of being a sports star. Australian sportsmen and women who reach the top of their fields are given a lot of attention by the media and some of them are paid lots of money.

While very few roles are available for professional sportspeople, there are many other ways to be professionally involved in sport.

WORK TYPES

KEY JOBS IN SPORT

- players
- coaches
- officiators
- sports managers
- sports administrators
- health and fitness experts
- sports teachers
- sports retailers
- sports and tourism operators

THINK AHEAD

If you think you might like a career in sport, there are things you can do now to help you get a job later on.

- keep playing sport
- get involved with a club, to be recognised for your contributions and achievements
- volunteer to help in a community sport
- talk to someone who is already doing the job that you're interested in
- find out what the job you're interested in actually involves

VOLUNTEERING

In Australia, more than three million people work in volunteer roles for sport and recreation organisations. Volunteering as a player, an official, a coach, a team manager or a secretary will help you better understand the sport you're interested in. Your experiences as a volunteer might also help you get a paid job later on.

MATCH YOUR INTERESTS

Choosing a job is not always easy. While all people want to be happy and involved in their work, everyone is interested in different things and each person has his or her own particular set of skills. Whatever your skills and talents are, if you want to work and be involved in sport, there are a range of interesting roles in the sports and recreation industry.

QUALIFICATIONS

A person becomes qualified for a job or a profession when he or she completes a course of study in an area relevant to that job or profession. Qualifications are important when looking for a job. Lots of TAFE colleges and universities offer courses that can help you prepare for the job you want. At TAFE colleges you can study for certificates, diplomas and degrees. At universities you can study for diplomas, bachelor's degrees and honours and masters degrees.

A PLAYING CAREER

Playing for love or playing for money?

The amount of money sportspeople earn each year depends on the sport they play and the level at which they play. An AFL footballer can earn over $350,000 a year while an equally successful softball player may only receive their expenses. Those sportsmen and women who get paid little or nothing play for the love of the sport and the honour of representing their club, state or country.

PROFESSIONAL SPORTSPERSON

JOB DESCRIPTION

Most young people play sport to keep fit and have fun, but some hope to go on and play the sport they love professionally. The sporting world is very competitive and to be the best requires talent, commitment and very hard work.

RANGE OF WORK:

- attend practice and training sessions
- participate in sporting competitions
- represent a club at official functions
- train privately to maintain fitness levels
- maintain sporting equipment

EDUCATION AND TRAINING

Sportspeople do not need formal educational qualifications to compete. However, some sports offer formal training programs to a small number of talented young players. Many promising sportspeople will also train at the Australian Institute of Sport (AIS) or at one of the state institutes of sport.

AFTER A PLAYING CAREER

Most sportspeople can only play at the top level for a limited number of years. This is because these roles are extremely competitive and new sportspeople are continually joining the field. Some sports-related jobs that top players go on to do include:

- sports coach
- sports commentator
- sports writer
- motivational speaker

MY STORY

I started playing netball when I was in primary school and I loved it right from the beginning. I played in local, district and regional teams and when I was 23 I was selected for the state team. I went to play for the Australian B team on a tour of New Zealand, which was a great experience. Later, I was asked to play for Singapore in the World Championships. It was the first time an Australian had played in a national netball team for another country.

You need to be very committed, flexible and organised to play for a state or national team because the time commitment is huge and you are paid very little or nothing at all. I've been a full-time teacher all the time I played netball and I had to combine this with training nearly every day and playing at the weekends.

For me, the best thing about playing netball has been the social aspect. I've made a huge number of friends all over Australia.

A few words of advice:
Make sure you are there for the enjoyment of the game and don't let anyone tell you that you won't make it.

JOCELYN BRYANT
NETBALL PLAYER

'Make sure you are there for the enjoyment of the game'

SUPPORTING SPORTSPEOPLE

For people who enjoy sport, there are jobs both on and off the field that support the players and athletes. These jobs involve working with players of all ages and abilities. They include:

- **sports officials**
- **player and team managers**
- **coaches**
- **sports lawyers**

COACH

JOB DESCRIPTION

Coaches work with individual sportspeople or with sporting teams to help them improve their performance. Coaches need good communication skills and a thorough understanding of their sports.

RANGE OF WORK:

- recruit players
- teach players new skills and improve existing skills
- plan team strategies
- plan and supervise training sessions
- attend games and give players instructions
- work with sports scientists
- liaise with sporting institutions
- perform administrative tasks

EDUCATION AND TRAINING

Tertiary education is not essential for coaching, but it could lead to greater opportunities. Experience playing the sport is advantageous. Many TAFE colleges offer courses in sport and recreation, and some universities offer coaching and sports administration as part of other courses.
The National Coaching Accreditation Scheme provides recognition of coaching qualifications.

MANAGER

JOB DESCRIPTION

A manager of a sportsperson or a sports team deals with the business side of sport. They require a good understanding of the game, great organisational and negotiation skills, and excellent communication skills.

RANGE OF WORK:

- help players with contracts with sports clubs
- help players with sponsorship
- arrange player's public appearances
- help players with career planning
- help players with money management

EDUCATION AND TRAINING

There are no educational requirements for going into the management field, but it helps to have qualifications in sports management. It also helps to have business and/or financial training or qualifications.

SPORTS OFFICIAL

JOB DESCRIPTION

Sports officials work as umpires, referees and judges. Many of these positions are voluntary, but the number of paid positions is growing. Sports officials need to be fit and have good concentration.

RANGE OF WORK:

- make sure the playing area is safe
- ensure play is safe and fair according to the rules
- settle arguments between players
- provide evidence to help resolve disputes

EDUCATION AND TRAINING

The National Officiating Accreditation Scheme provides support for sports officials.. All officials must be registered with the National Officiating Accreditation Scheme.

'you can … begin by coaching juniors'

MY STORY

I was 16 when I began playing hockey, which is quite late. I started coaching juniors when I was 17. I really enjoyed coaching so I coached senior players while I studied to be a social worker. My experience as a youth worker helped my coaching and I went on to be a trainer and then assistant coach with the Victorian Men's Hockey Team. Then I coached the Victorian Women's Hockey team. Now I'm back coaching the Victorian Men's team as well as being Head Coach of the Victorian Institute of Sports' Hockey Program. One of the best things about my job is watching players develop as individuals, as well as sportspeople.

A few words of advice:
You can come to coaching as a high profile player, but you can also begin by coaching juniors.

JOHN MOWAT
HEAD COACH

SPORT AND THE MEDIA

The term *sports media* covers sports reporting for newspapers, magazines, radio, television and the Internet. Roles in sports media include:

- sports journalist
- sports photographer
- sports commentator
- sports program producer
- sports editor

SPORTS COMMENTATOR

JOB DESCRIPTION

Sports commentators work on both radio and television. They comment on the sport as it is being played, to enhance the spectator's experience.

RANGE OF WORK:

- attend and comment on sporting events
- describe exactly what happens during sporting events
- analyse the sporting performances and events afterwards
- interview people

EDUCATION AND TRAINING

There are no educational requirements, but commentators need a thorough knowledge of the sport.

• SPORTS JOURNALIST

JOB DESCRIPTION

Sports journalists need to have an interest in sport and an ability to write well to a deadline. They work for television, newspapers, magazines and online outlets.

RANGE OF WORK:

- attend sporting events and report on what happens
- comment on what else is happening in that particular sport, from the pre-season training to the final event of the year
- write about the sport, the players, the coaches and the venues

EDUCATION AND TRAINING

Media outlets such as the ABC sometimes train their journalists through cadetships, but very few cadetships are offered and the competition for them is fierce. Many journalists have a degree in journalism or media, or a diploma in journalism or professional writing.

• WEBSITE DEVELOPER

JOB DESCRIPTION

Sporting websites give up-to-date information on different sports. People who work in this area must have good writing abilities, good organisational skills and the technical knowledge to create the website.

RANGE OF WORK:

- design sports websites
- decide on content and its presentation
- ensure smooth, intuitive online user experience
- keep the site up-to-date

EDUCATION AND TRAINING

Website developers often have TAFE or university qualifications in graphic or web design. A strong sporting knowledge base is the most important factor although the job will require experience with different software and coding languages.

MY STORY

I left uni halfway through an Arts degree and got a job as a copy boy at a newspaper. I was lucky to get a cadetship as they only took four out of 450 applicants. I started off doing everything from the auction results to the police rounds, but I loved sport – particularly footy. I played footy, cricket and golf, so it was good to be able to write about them. Now I'm football editor at The Australian and the golf writer for the paper. I cover everything, from the games to the training sessions and the tribunal. I love sport and the excitement when a story breaks. There's a strong sense of being at the centre of everything when you work on a newspaper. I also get to travel a lot and cover international tournaments. The downside is that we often work late getting the stories ready for the next day's paper.

A few words of advice:
Be prepared to start anywhere – you could even write for your school magazine!

MICHAEL DAVIES
SENIOR SPORTS WRITER

'Be prepared to start anywhere'

SPORT, HEALTH AND FITNESS

Health and fitness is a growing industry in Australia. As people are learning more about nutrition and health issues, they are becoming more aware of the importance of keeping fit. Some people pay instructors and trainers to help them keep in shape. Fitness instructors concentrate more on physical fitness activities than sporting games. These physical fitness activities might include yoga, weightlifting or even gymnastics.

• YOGA INSTRUCTOR

JOB DESCRIPTION

Yoga is a strengthening form of controlled exercise, designed to improve the body's stamina, strength, circulation and oxygen intake. Yoga instructors need to have a good level of fitness and strong communication skills. They also need to enjoy working with people.

RANGE OF WORK:

- plan yoga routines
- assess clients' needs and fitness levels
- order and maintain equipment
- take classes and record online tutorials

EDUCATION AND TRAINING

To become Yoga Australia certified, you can complete training through a Yoga Australia accredited school. Most yoga teacher training schools focus on different aspects of yoga.

• CHILDREN'S GYM INSTRUCTOR

JOB DESCRIPTION

Fitness is not just for adults. Many fitness centres offer gym programs for toddlers and children. Children's gym instructors need to have lots of patience, good communication skills and be able to work as part of a team.

RANGE OF WORK:

- assess individual children's needs
- plan exercise programs
- plan and organise movement games
- design group activities

EDUCATION AND TRAINING

Children's gym instructors often have qualifications in child development as well as a certificate or diploma in fitness or physical education. Fitness qualifications are most important, as well as a valid Working with Children Check. Training specific to instructing children may be provided on the job.

• PERSONAL TRAINER

JOB DESCRIPTION

With millions of people wanting to lose weight and get in shape all over the country, personal training is a fast-growing career. Job opportunities for personal trainers can be found at health and fitness clubs, gymnasiums, resorts and even on cruise ships. Many personal trainers also start their own businesses.

RANGE OF WORK:

- plan workout programs
- give advice on lifestyle and nutrition
- motivate clients to achieve their personal best
- monitor client's progress

EDUCATION AND TRAINING

Becoming a personal trainer usually requires a certificate, diploma or traineeship. Entry requirements to these courses vary. Instructors should also be registered according to the rules of their particular state.

MY STORY

I'd always played a lot of sport at school but I hadn't thought of sport or exercise as a career. Actually, I wasn't sure what I wanted to do when I left school after finishing Year 12. While I was thinking about it, I bought myself a gym membership and a good weight set and went into training.

When I saw what this did for me, I thought about training other people. I got my qualifications and registration, specialising in fitness instruction, and decided to set up my own business.

I advertised and, because I didn't have much money, I started off with a mobile business going to people's houses. Now I've got a studio and a partner and our business is gradually growing.

I really like this job. I like meeting people and being able to work with them on equal terms. The only thing I don't really like is when people don't take their fitness seriously and blame the trainer for their lack of progress.

A few words of advice:
Give it a go and remember that 75 per cent of this sort of job is relating to people and understanding what they need.

JAMES KILLEN
PERSONAL TRAINER

'75 per cent of this sort of job is relating to people'

SPORT AND SCIENCE

The field of sports science includes medicine, physiology, psychology, physiotherapy, biomechanics and nutrition. Job opportunities in these areas are growing all the time.

• SPORTS SCIENTIST

JOB DESCRIPTION

Sports scientists help sportspeople to achieve their best possible sporting performance. They perform fitness tests on athletes to determine how their bodies work to help them develop ways to maximise their performance. Sports scientists also work to ensure athletes' bodies are moving smoothly in order to prevent injuries.

RANGE OF SPECIALITIES:

- ***medicine*** – treating injuries and illness
- ***physiology*** – improving how the body works
- ***nutrition*** – providing the best foods and supplements for high performance
- ***psychology*** – working on mental preparations
- ***biomechanics*** – analysing and improving body movements

EDUCATION AND TRAINING

Sports scientists need a degree in applied science, human movement science, or exercise/sports science.

• SPORTS DIETITIAN

JOB DESCRIPTION

Sports dietitians apply the science of nutrition to help elite sportspeople perform at their best. Sports dietitians plan diets for sportspeople and educate them on how to prepare meals.

EDUCATION AND TRAINING

To become a dietitian you need a degree in nutrition and dietetics. As it is a competitive field, most sports dietitians have postgraduate qualifications. Dietitians with lots of experience working with athletes are considered sports dietitians, although you may also specialise in sports nutrition at postgraduate level.

SPORTS PSYCHOLOGIST

JOB DESCRIPTION

Sports psychologists work with athletes to ensure they are mentally prepared for elite competition. They usually work with individual athletes though they can work with a team.

RANGE OF WORK:

- advise on ways to improve concentration
- advise on stress management
- advise on ways to achieve positive thinking
- advise on how to perform under pressure

EDUCATION AND TRAINING

Sport psychologists need to complete a degree in psychology. Most positions will require a postgraduate psychology degree with an emphasis on sports psychology.

SPORTS PHYSIOTHERAPIST

JOB DESCRIPTION

Sports physiotherapists treat muscle, tendon and ligament injuries.

RANGE OF WORK:

- diagnose problems
- treat patients with massage, heat and exercises
- give advice to prevent injuries and problems

EDUCATION AND TRAINING

Sports physiotherapists must complete a degree in physiotherapy and specialise in sporting injuries. Physiotherapists must register with the Physiotherapy Board of Australia

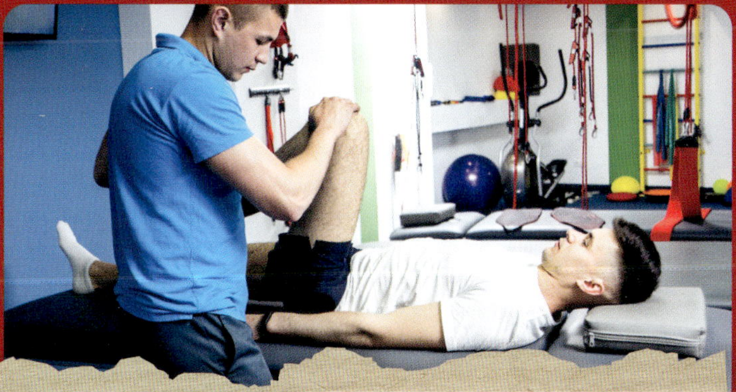

MY STORY

I'm researching the ways in which sportspeople make decisions as they play. We find out what information each player uses to make a decision and work out how effective his or her decision making is. We need to make sure that in the seconds it takes to decide what to do with the ball that players are only looking at what is important. I also develop computer software that helps athletes improve their skills.

I really like the variety of my job and the contact with sport, and there is plenty of opportunity for international travel at this level. The downside is lots of early mornings and late nights as this is when many athletes train. It's a difficult job to fit in with family life. There are plenty of opportunities to work overseas, as Australian sports scientists are always wanted, particularly in the UK and Canada.

A few words of advice:
Study hard, get involved in sporting clubs and get experience.

STUART MORGAN
SPORTS SCIENTIST

'There are plenty of opportunities to work overseas'

SPORT AND RECREATION

There are lots of different recreational sporting venues all around Australia. Ice-skating rinks, ten-pin bowling alleys, swimming pools, rock-climbing centres and indoor-cricket centres are just some of the sporting facilities available. These venues are both for people who want some exercise and fun, as well as for people who play sport competitively.

• RECREATIONAL VENUE MANAGER

JOB DESCRIPTION

A manager's job will depend on the type of recreational facility he or she is managing.

RANGE OF WORK:

- hire and supervise staff
- organise rosters
- supervise the maintenance of the building
- organise promotions, competitions and tournaments
- make sure the centre offers something to people of different ages and abilities

EDUCATION AND TRAINING

Managers need organisation and communication skills. Although formal qualifications are not necessary, a diploma or a degree in marketing and/or management will open up greater career opportunities.

• ACTIVITY INSTRUCTOR

JOB DESCRIPTION

Activity instructors teach people how to take part in sporting activities safely.

RANGE OF WORK:

- teach sporting skills
- maintain equipment
- plan activities and exercises
- supervise activities to makes sure they are completed safely

EDUCATION AND TRAINING

Formal qualifications are not always essential, but a certificate or diploma in sport and recreation, a degree in physical education and/or teaching qualifications would help with this job.

• LIFEGUARD

JOB DESCRIPTION

Public swimming pools are patrolled by professional lifeguards, whose jobs involve supervising people in the water. Many of the Surf Life Savers who patrol Australian beaches are trained volunteers, but there are also people in paid positions who work in water safety. Lifeguards must be physically fit, have good concentration and good communication skills.

RANGE OF WORK:

- monitor the water quality
- make sure conditions are safe for everyone
- supervise swimmers
- keep rescue equipment in good order
- rescue people in difficulties
- provide first aid when necessary

EDUCATION AND TRAINING

A pool lifeguard must have a First Aid Certificate and complete a pool lifeguard training certificate.
The minimum requirement for a Surf Life Saver is the Bronze Medallion (Certificate II in Aquatic Rescue) in addition to certificates in advanced resuscitation techniques and first aid. These are awarded by the Surf Life Saving Association. Surf Life Savers can train beyond this and gain their Silver Medallion (Patrol Captain) and their Gold Medallion (Advanced Life Saving).

'Get some qualifications in business or marketing'

MY STORY

I've bowled since I was a kid, and when I was 21, I walked into a bowling centre and asked for a job. I started behind the desk, taking the money and dealing with shoe hire and gradually worked my way up to managing my own centre. I now employ around 42 staff, but still have to know what is going on in every area – in the creche, behind the bar, in the bowling alleys and behind the front desk.

I like the fact that no two days are the same. It's also good working for an international company – you can apply for jobs anywhere in Australia or even overseas. The downside is the working hours – when everyone else is relaxing, I'm working hardest.

A few words of advice:
Get some qualifications in business or marketing but find casual work at a venue at the same time.

ROD EAST
BOWLING CENTRE MANAGER

SPORTING CLUBS

Nearly four million Australians play sport as members of clubs or associations. Thousands of people also belong to clubs as social members. There are clubs for almost every sport, ranging from athletics to lawn bowls. These clubs provide employment in a number of different areas.

CLUB PROFESSIONAL

JOB DESCRIPTION

Club professionals are paid by clubs to run the pro shop and provide coaching to club members. The club professional has the same kind of job, no matter what sport he or she plays.

RANGE OF WORK:

- teach beginners
- help others improve their game
- offer sporting advice
- run the pro shop

EDUCATION AND TRAINING

The Professional Golf Association (PGA) runs a number of training programs. Trainee golf professionals also study business management at a university.

RECEPTIONIST

JOB DESCRIPTION

Most clubs employ a receptionist to handle phone calls and enquiries. A receptionist is often the first person someone contacts at the club, so it's important for this person to have very good communication skills.

RANGE OF WORK:

- greet and show people around the club
- deal with enquiries and provide information
- arrange appointments
- keep the office well organised
- perform clerical duties

EDUCATION AND TRAINING

Not all receptionists have formal qualifications, but job opportunities are increased with an accredited certificate in business or office administration. These are available through TAFE colleges.

WORKING WITH A TEAM

A large club will have a management team that might include:

- facility managers, who look after the club's facilities
- marketing managers, who look after things like sponsorship and advertising
- financial managers, who manage the club's finances
- human resource managers, who support the staff employed by the club
- public relations managers, who look after the relationship between the club, its members and the public

GROUNDS AND MAINTENANCE STAFF

All sporting clubs have facilities, such as the club's buildings and grounds, that need to be looked after. A grounds and maintenance team might include:

- curators
- greenkeepers
- gardeners
- cleaners
- general maintenance staff

MY STORY

I started playing golf when I was a kid and being a golf pro is what I've always wanted to do. I have to play 30 tournaments a year to keep my average up, but it's the teaching I enjoy. My job includes working in the pro shop and coaching club members who are learning or who want to brush up on their technique. I'm still training, so I have to do a bit of everything. Later on I'll be able to choose between working in the pro shop and teaching.

I'm studying business management by correspondence at Griffith University and I'm doing a trainee program run by the Professional Golf Association.

A few words of advice:
Play your sport as much as you can. Don't let people tell you that you can't do it!

DARREN ROWLAND
TRAINEE GOLF CLUB PROFESSIONAL

'Play your sport as much as you can'

SPORT AND TEACHING

• TEACHING IN SCHOOLS

JOB DESCRIPTION

Australian high schools and many primary schools employ trained physical education (PE) teachers to instruct students in sports, recreational activities and lifestyle issues.

RANGE OF WORK:

- plan and prepare a teaching program for the year
- teach the basic techniques of a range of individual and team sports
- teach students about personal and community health
- teach students about personal development
- coordinate special sporting events like athletics and swimming carnivals
- teach students safety practices on the sporting field and in the water

EDUCATION AND TRAINING

PE teachers need to complete a four-year degree in education, or a degree followed by a Graduate Diploma of Education. Special training and qualifications might be needed for some activities, such as swimming.

PRIVATE COACHING

JOB DESCRIPTION

Some sportspeople give private lessons in sports such as tennis and swimming. These coaches usually work through a club or a sports centre. Sometimes people set up their own small businesses.

EDUCATION AND TRAINING

Although coaching qualifications are not strictly necessary to set up as a coach, if you want to be part of a club and use their facilities you will need to have coaching qualifications.

'make sure you get your coaching qualifications'

MY STORY

I've played tennis for as long as I can remember and was working as an assistant coach by the time I was 15. I coached kids while I was studying media arts as a way of earning some money and because I enjoyed it. I'm not a registered coach so I can't work at a tennis club. I have to find courts to use and build up my business through my own efforts. I have to run things like a business. There's all the paperwork, sending out accounts, chasing up the money people owe, coping with the GST and ringing around organising lesson times.

Coaching is not just about teaching tennis skills – it's about helping kids learn how to win and lose while still enjoying the game. I really like working with all sorts of kids and watching them improve their own particular game. The only real problem with the job is that you are so dependent on the weather.

A few words of advice:
This is a really rewarding job but, if you want to do it full-time, make sure you get your coaching qualifications, become registered as a coach and build your business through a tennis club.

BEN LEVESON
TENNIS COACH

SPORTING VENUES AND EVENTS

Australians have always loved watching sport and football finals can attract huge crowds. Sports stadiums are often designed to be multi-purpose, and seating arrangements and playing surfaces can be changed to suit the sport or purpose. Sometimes venues are adapted for concerts, ice skating and even dance performances.

EVENT MANAGERS

JOB DESCRIPTION

Major events involve huge numbers of people, including the participants, the audience, the sponsors, the media, the paid staff and the volunteers. Event managers are responsible for coordinating all these groups of people. This kind of job calls for excellent planning, organisation and communication skills, as well as the ability to work as part of a team.

RANGE OF WORK:

- prepare budgets
- promote events
- deal with sponsors
- organise catering
- coordinate advertising, signage, ticketing and parking

EDUCATION AND TRAINING

Event managers can complete a Diploma of Event Management which is typically a full-time course over one year. Alternatively, complete a Bachelor of Business (Event Management), which is usually full-time for three years.

CATERERS

JOB DESCRIPTION

The catering for sporting events is usually done by companies that specialise in major event hospitality.

RANGE OF ROLES:

- *catering staff* – plan menus and prepare and deliver food
- *bar staff* – take orders for drinks, pour and serve drinks and clear away glasses
- *waiting staff* – welcome customers, take orders, and serve food and drinks

EDUCATION AND TRAINING

For these jobs, it's possible to get qualifications at TAFEs through certificates or diplomas in all different kinds of food preparation. However, they are often not needed. Anyone serving alcohol needs an RSA certificate.

CORPORATE MANAGERS

JOB DESCRIPTION

Major events call for special financial and legal knowledge. Such roles might include:

- finance managers, who oversee financial arrangements such as contracts
- accountants and bookkeepers, who make records of financial transactions, prepare regular financial reports and manage accounts

EDUCATION AND TRAINING

Universities and TAFE colleges offer a wide range of courses in commerce, business and management. A background in sports or event administration would also be helpful.

'You need to have qualifications in management'

MY STORY

I studied public relations and human resource management and I started working here as a casual. I worked my way up to this position. There's nothing like doing your training on the job.

My job involves coordinating the full-time, part-time and casual work force. I deal with hiring and rostering of a huge casual work force, staff training and preparation for major events.

I really like the excitement and variety of my job. You never know what you are going to be called on to deal with next.

A few words of advice:
This is a very competitive area to work in. We had over 400 applicants for two coordinating positions recently. You need to have qualifications in management, as well as commitment and persistence.

CORINNE KROGH
HUMAN RESOURCES

SPORT AND THE COMMUNITY

Sport plays a big part in Australian communities and most people will become involved in sport at some time in their lives. This is not only good for their health, it also helps create stronger communities. People get to know each other as they play for and support their local teams.

JUNIOR SPORTS

JOB DESCRIPTION

Almost two million children play some kind of sport outside school hours. Inter-club basketball, netball, hockey and football are just some of the sports which are played every Saturday throughout the school year. National programs such as the Surf Life Saving Association's Nipper program are run all over Australia and organised at a local level. While much of the work done is voluntary, there are some paid positions available in coaching and management.

RANGE OF OPPORTUNITIES:

- working for State or Federal Governments setting up and promoting recreational programs and facilities
- making links with sporting organisations and communities
- developing programs and the infrastructure to support them

WORK IN COMMUNITY SPORTS:

- regional and district management
- promotion and coordination of programs
- officiating at games
- coaching teams

• WORKING AT A LOCAL LEVEL

Local councils own most of the sporting fields and facilities in Australia. Clubs and sporting associations hire courts, ovals and other facilities, or work with local councils to keep them running. Councils often support community sporting clubs and organisations and employ sport and recreation officers to promote a healthy lifestyle in the community.

• WORKING AT A STATE AND FEDERAL LEVEL

Federal and State governments have ministers who are responsible for sport and recreation. People in their departments work with a range of sporting organisations in order to:

- form policies on sport and recreation
- build important sporting facilities
- organise major sporting events
- develop the sport and tourism industry

MY STORY

I'm the link between the Surf Life Saving Association and the community. I organise community education courses through schools, leadership and youth development camps, and through the Nipper program. This is a program that teaches kids to be safe in the water and encourages them to take on a role in the Surf Life Saving Association.

I began as a Nipper myself and became involved in the Surf Life Saving Association doing voluntary work and later as a paid lifeguard. I've got all the association awards including my Gold Medallion. I'm also studying for a Bachelor of Business and Marketing.

This job calls for knowledge of the association from the ground upwards and reasonable computer skills. You also need a good understanding of teamwork.

I like working with young people and I love the fact that I'm not stuck in an office all the time. I'm always meeting new people, which is great.

A few words of advice:
Get tertiary qualifications in sports management or sports administration. Become involved on a voluntary basis because one thing leads to another.

DAVID MORGAN
DEVELOPMENT MANAGER
SURF LIFE SAVING

'Become involved on a voluntary basis'

SPORT AND TOURISM

Sport-related tourism is very popular in Australia. People often look to combine their enjoyment of sport with their holidays.

• KIDS' ADVENTURE CAMPS

JOB DESCRIPTION

People who are interested in outdoor recreation and enjoy working with children of all ages, might want to consider working at a holiday adventure camp. This sort of work is often casual or part-time, but it gives people valuable experience. Anyone working in this area has to have patience, good communication skills, a reasonable level of fitness and an ability to get on well with staff and kids.

RANGE OF JOBS:

- *outdoor recreation instructors* – teach outdoor recreation activities, such as horse riding, kayaking, rafting and rock climbing
- *activity leaders* – plan, organise and lead activities
- *camp coordinators* – answer enquiries, take bookings, oversee the camp, talk to parents, supervise staff and organise programs and staff rosters
- *camp cooks* – order food supplies and cook meals

EDUCATION AND TRAINING

Not all these jobs require qualifications, and much of the training is done on the job. But in the case of teaching high risk sports, such as abseiling or white-water rafting, instructors will need at least a certificate in that particular activity. A qualification in sport and recreation, or in outdoor recreation, will also increase chances of employment.

• ALPINE EMPLOYMENT

JOB DESCRIPTION

During the ski season there are many jobs available at ski resorts. Nearly all jobs at ski resorts are about dealing with the public, so they call for good communication skills, an outgoing nature and an enjoyment of winter conditions.

RANGE OF JOBS:

- ski/snowboard instructors
- chefs, bar staff and wait staff
- housekeepers and childcare workers
- maintenance staff
- ski lift operators
- ski shop assistants

Many of these jobs will last only for the season, but often include accommodation, meals and ski hire.

EDUCATION AND TRAINING

Most of these jobs require no formal qualifications and training is given on the job. Ski resorts usually have their own training program for ski and snowboard instructors but demand a certain standard from staff before offering training.

• ADVENTURE TOURISM

JOB DESCRIPTION

Adventure tourism is growing rapidly in Australia. Adventure tourism covers all sorts of different holiday experiences but generally involves challenging outdoor activities. These extreme kinds of activities include exciting sports such as skydiving, bungee jumping and white-water rafting. Sports like these need trained leaders to supervise them. TAFE colleges offer qualifications in outdoor recreation.

MY STORY

I've always loved skiing but it's a very expensive sport. One way to get a season's skiing is to work as a chef during the ski season. I've done this at a few resorts now and I really love it. I did an apprenticeship in hospitality and I've worked in restaurants and hotels all over the place, but I love the atmosphere at the snow.

You have to work pretty hard and you can't always choose which shift you do, but there's enough time off to go skiing. You get to meet heaps of people and everyone is always very social. There are no downsides to this job, except that you have to find something else to do for the rest of the year.

A few words of advice:
Look up the resort on the net and get in early with your job application. There are lots of people who want to work at the snow!

JANE RUSSELL
CHEF

'get in early with your job application'

SPORT AND RETAIL

As more people get involved in sport, they demand a wider range of sporting goods. Sporting goods are the pieces of equipment, the clothes and the shoes that are used in any kind of sport or exercise. Sport retailing, the selling of sporting goods to the public, is a growing area of employment. All sports products are designed, manufactured and advertised before they are ready to sell. The people who work in these areas need very different skills.

• DESIGNER

JOB DESCRIPTION

Designers work with athletes to create sporting equipment that will help them improve their performance. They also work to design sporting products for people who exercise for fun.

RANGE OF WORK:

- think about the needs of the manufacturer and/or the client
- research and develop a product
- consider things like cost, fashion and safety
- make sketches and prototypes of the product
- estimate the cost of production

EDUCATION AND TRAINING

The education and training a designer needs depends on his or her area of design. A sportswear designer needs a diploma or degree in fashion design, but a designer of sporting equipment might need a degree in industrial design.

• RETAILER

JOB DESCRIPTION

The growing area of health and fitness has created a growth in sports retailing. Sports retailing is when sporting products are sold to the general public through retail outlets.

RANGE OF WORK:

- retail managers – oversee the sports shop or sports department, supervise staff, organise rosters, keep records of sales figures and deal with sales representatives
- retail buyers – decide which products will sell, research different products, order stock and deal with suppliers
- sales assistants – advise customers on location, choice and availability of goods, take payment for goods, take orders for goods and organise stock on the floor

EDUCATION AND TRAINING

Becoming a sales assistant, manager or buyer requires no formal qualifications and training is usually done on the job. Managers and buyers often start off as sales assistants.

• ADVERTISER

JOB DESCRIPTION

Advertisers plan advertising campaigns. They decide on what sort of advertisements to use and where to place them.

RANGE OF WORK:

- research the product
- find out who will buy the product
- generate ideas for advertisements
- coordinate advertising campaigns

EDUCATION AND TRAINING

Working as an advertiser usually requires a degree or diploma in marketing or advertising.

MY STORY

I've always played sport, particularly golf, and that's how I got the job here. I met someone on the golf course who was managing the store and he needed someone who knew about golf and tennis.

The job involves a bit of everything. I organise the stock, which means making sure everything that is needed is out on the shop floor and kept in order. I serve customers – advising them on what they need, answering their questions and being there whenever they need help. We sell equipment for nearly every sport, but I specialise in tennis and golf.

You don't need any formal qualifications to work in a sports store, but it helps to have a strong knowledge of a particular sport and a good general knowledge of sport. You also really need to get on well with people.

A few words of advice:
Play the sport you are interested in so you can keep up with what's happening in that area. Talk to everyone - you never know who might help you get a job.

RYAN PRATT
SALES ASSISTANT

'The job involves a bit of everything'

GET FUTURE READY

If you think you might be interested in a career in sports, there are a few things that you can do right now that might be useful later. Why not research your education pathways to see what options are available to you? Maybe you could plan the qualification route that you might like to follow, or investigate the practical steps you could take to gain experience in the types of work that interest you.

• THE FUTURE

PRACTICAL EXPERIENCE

- get involved in sporting clubs so that you can gain insight into your preferred sporting area
- volunteer with your local club to gain experience and make potential work contacts
- talk to people who work in similar roles to those you are interested in
- read as much as you can about the job
- check what qualifications are needed
- research the job on the Internet

DO YOU NEED QUALIFICATIONS?

There are many different levels of qualifications and training opportunities for jobs in sport. Some jobs in sport can be entered into straight from secondary school, while some require TAFE certificates, diplomas and sometimes a university degree. Sports scientists will have postgraduate qualifications and specialisations in their fields. The sports industry is competitive, so the more qualifications you have, the more likely you are to get a job in your chosen area.

GLOSSARY

accredited meeting the official requirements

administration management of a business

cadetship formal period of training while working on a newspaper

communication skills ability to listen, express yourself and understand other people

contract legal agreement

coverage reporting of an event by the media

facility building or structure with an assortment of areas that facilitate an activity

infrastructure buildings and facilities that are needed to provide access to services

lecturer someone who delivers a class, usually at a university or TAFE

local council group of elected people who form a Local Government

manufacturer someone who makes something, usually in a factory

media modes of communication including television, newspapers, radio and the Internet

National Officiating Accreditation sets standards which officials must reach to be registered at a particular level

National Coaching Accreditation Scheme sets standards which coaches must reach to qualify at a particular level

negotiation attempt to reach an agreement on something through compromise

nutrition study of food and how it affects our bodies

officiators people who run a game

organisational skills ability to organise yourself and any jobs you have to do

physiology science of living things and their parts

physiotherapy treatment of injury through heat, exercise and massage

promotion publicising and selling of a product

pro shop shop at a sports club that sells equipment to play that sport

psychology scientific study of the human mind

retail outlet shop that sells to the public

roster plan, like a diary, showing when staff members will be working and what they will be doing over a particular period of time

sponsorship when organisations fund sportspeople, teams or clubs in return for advertising

sports official someone who ensures a sporting event is conducted safely and according to the rules

syllabus subjects to be studied in a particular course

TAFE Technical And Further Education

tertiary formal education beyond secondary school

wholesalers those who sell bulk quantities of product to retailers, who then sell it to the public

INDEX